EARTH & SPACE SCIENCES

Looking at Our Changing Earth

by
Alan Venable

Don Johnston Incorporated
Volo, Illinois

Edited by:

John Bergez
Start-to-Finish Core Content Series Editor, Pacifica, California

Barbara Armentrout, MA
Start-to-Finish Core Content Developmental Editor, San Carlos, California

Gail Portnuff Venable, MS, CCC-SLP
Speech/Language Pathologist, San Francisco, California

Dorothy Tyack, MA
Learning Disabilities Specialist, San Francisco, California

Jerry Stemach, MS, CCC-SLP
Speech/Language Pathologist, Director of Content Development, Sonoma County, California

Graphics and Illustrations:

Photographs and illustrations are all created professionally and modified to provide the best possible support for the intended reader.
Page 7 and back cover: Courtesy of the Illinois State Museum Society
Page 11: Courtesy of the US Army Corps of Engineers, New Orleans District
Page 12: Rocardo Saraiva - FOTOLIA
Page 13: © Marli Bryant Miller
Page 20: University Museums, University of Delaware, Newark, DE, given by Peter Frorer
Page 21: © Studio Araminta, 2007. Used under license from Shutterstock.com.
Page 22: Courtesy of the USGS
Page 23: © Steve Lovegrove - FOTOLIA and © iStockphoto.com/Don Wilke
Page 25: Courtesy of the Kentucky Geological Survey, University of Kentucky
Page 31: © IODP/TAMU
Page 33: © iStockphoto.com/Scott Spencer
Page 34: © National Park Service
Page 35: Ilya D. Gridnev, 2007. Used under license from Shutterstock.com.
Page 38: © NASA/JPL/NIMA
Page 39: © NASA
Page 40: © Terry Morris - FOTOLIA
Page 42 and back cover: Courtesy of the USDA, Photo by Jeff Vanuga
All other photos not credited here or with the photo are © Don Johnston Incorporated and its licensors.

Narration:

Professional actors and actresses read the text to build excitement and to model research-based elements of fluency: intonation, stress, prosody, phrase groupings and rate. The rate has been set to maximize comprehension for the reader.

Published by:

Don Johnston Incorporated
26799 West Commerce Drive
Volo, IL 60073

800.999.4660 USA Canada
800.889.5242 Technical Support
www.donjohnston.com

International Standard Book Number
ISBN 978-1-4105-0996-3

Table of Contents

Introduction: Going to Look for Rocks

When you look at a mountain, you might think it has always been there. And you might think it always *will* be there. But you would be wrong. The surface of Earth is always changing. Today, new mountains are rising up while older mountains are being worn away. Somewhere, land at the bottom of the sea is rising up to form new mountains. Somewhere else, dry land is slowly washing into the sea.

Old mountains like these are slowly wearing away.

This book will help you look at Earth in new ways. A scientist named Rockhound will be your guide. Rockhound wants to find out why Earth is always changing. He studies the science of Earth and its rocks. This science is called **geology**. And Rockhound is a **geologist**.

Today, you and Rockhound are out in some dry, rocky hills. You are both down in a pit that Rockhound has dug in the ground. Rockhound sees something in the side of the pit, so he hands you his favorite tool for geology. It's a rock hammer.

Rockhound points at a rock with his rock hammer.

Rockhound shows you where to start digging.

You use the pointed end of the hammer to dig a rock out of the wall of dirt.

"This rock is so round!" you say. "What is it?"

"Here's a hint," he says. "The word for this rock begins with *g-e-o* just like the word *geology*."

"*Geo-*?" you ask. "Doesn't *geo-* mean 'Earth'?"

"Right," he says. "This rock is a **geode**, which means 'shaped like Earth.' "

Rockhound gives you another tool that geologists use. It's a magnifying glass. Now you look more closely at the geode through the lens of the magnifying glass.

"I see a small hole in this rock," you say. "It looks like there's a tiny cave in there."

"Now hit the rock with the hammer," says Rockhound.

You set the geode on another rock, and you hit it with the hammer. It splits apart. You look at the broken pieces. The geode is hollow and there is another kind of rock inside. The rock inside the geode is white and it sparkles.

"Wow," you say. "I didn't expect to see this!"

"Those are crystals inside the rock," Rockhound says. "And they are millions of years old. When you opened the geode with the rock hammer, you became the first person to ever see those crystals! But I'll tell you more about crystals later. Right now, we have other interesting things to discover."

Rockhound has let you use his rock hammer and magnifying glass. In this book, you will learn about some other tools that may surprise you. As you learn about the tools that are used by geologists, you will also learn about Earth and its rocks.

This geode has been split apart. You can see the crystals inside it.

Chapter One

Hutton's Hammer: How the Science of Geology Began

Questions this chapter will answer:

- **What did the first geologists look at?**
- **What did they learn about the surface of Earth?**
- **What did James Hutton find out about the age of Earth? And how old is Earth really?**

At his office, Rockhound has a picture on the wall.

"Who is that?" you ask one day.

"That's my hero," says Rockhound. "His name is James Hutton. He started the science of geology. Hutton was the first person to figure out that Earth was very, very old. Hutton was born in Scotland in 1726. Back then, many people thought that Earth was only a few thousand years old. Today, we know that Earth is more than four and a half billion years old."

James Hutton with his rock hammer

"How did Hutton figure out that Earth was really old?" you ask.

"Well," Rockhound says, "a few scientists began to look carefully at the surface of Earth. Hutton was one of these scientists. He walked all over Britain and Europe studying rocks. His main tool was a rock hammer. Everywhere he went, Hutton broke off pieces of rock to study."

What did Hutton and the other geologists look at? How did they figure out that Earth was more than just a few thousand years old? This chapter will answer these questions.

What the First Geologists Looked At

Hutton and others looked at rivers and riverbanks (the ground on the sides of rivers). They saw that bits of dirt from the riverbanks got washed away as rivers flowed along. The bits of dirt were then carried along as muddy water. In this way, the rivers were **eroding** (wearing away) their banks. Then Hutton looked downstream and saw that the bits of dirt were sinking to the bottom of the river, which is called the river bed. These bits of dirt in water are called **sediment**. Hutton saw that the sediment had piled up into layers of mud on the river bed.

A flood eroded the bank of this river. The water is muddy because it is filled with sediment.

Hutton wanted to see what was under Earth's top layers of soil, so he looked at the walls of high cliffs by the ocean. Strong waves had worn away the sides of these cliffs, so he could see layers of rock in them. Hutton also looked down into deep mines. In these mines and cliffs, he could see a few hundred feet down into Earth's crust. The crust is the rocky outside layer of Earth. In some places, the crust is 50 miles (80 kilometers) deep.

What the First Geologists Learned

Hutton and other geologists could see enough of Earth's crust to understand some important facts. First, they could see that Earth's crust was made of layers of rock. They called these layers **strata**. They also saw that some strata had bits of seashells in them. The shells were in a kind of light-colored rock called **limestone**. Hutton and his friends found limestone all over Britain. They figured that the limestone strata with the seashells must have been formed long ago from sediment at the bottom of a sea. But these strata were miles away from the sea and high above it, too, so how did the seashells get into the limestone? Hutton guessed that there must have once been a sea where the limestone was now.

Seashell in a limestone rock

Hutton and his friends got new ideas from these facts. For example, they decided that some layers or strata must be older than others. How did they know? In many places, they found the limestone under a layer of **sandstone**. Sandstone is rock that began as a layer of sand. The limestone was under the sandstone, so the limestone had to be older than the sandstone. In this way, the strata told the history of changes on Earth.

Photo A shows ripples made by ocean water on beach sand. Photo B shows ripples in sandstone that was beach sand 200 million years ago.

The geologists also noticed that some strata were not flat. The strata must have started out as sediment and then turned into flat strata of rock over millions of years, but now, some of the strata were not flat any more — they were bent. The strata had been pushed up in some places and pulled down in other places. The geologists saw that this pushing and pulling had formed hills and mountains.

Layers of rock were pushed up to make these mountains.

Hutton's New Idea about the Age of Earth

Before Hutton, most people believed that the surface of Earth had never changed very much. They saw that some strata were being worn down by wind and water, but they did not believe that new strata were building up. Hutton had a different idea. Hutton saw that new strata were building up at the same time as older strata were being worn down. New rock strata were being built up by sediment. New rock strata were also being built up by the red-hot rock that pours out of volcanoes.

From all this, Hutton knew that Earth must be very old. Why? Because Earth's crust has hundreds of strata of rock in some places, and it must have taken thousands of years for *each layer* of sediment to turn into rock. To make Earth's crust, many slow changes must have happened, over and over, many times. Hutton could not guess exactly how old Earth was, but he knew that it had to be millions and millions of years old. Today, scientists know that Earth is even older than that. Earth is more than four and a half billion years old.

It took millions of years to make these strata.

Chapter Summary

In this chapter, you learned that James Hutton was the founder of geology. In the 1700s, Hutton and other people began to study Earth's crust. They saw that water eroded rock and that water helped to form sediment. Over time, this sediment turned into strata of rock. Hills and mountains rose up in the places where the strata became bent. The strata formed a history of Earth's crust.

Hutton said that Earth's surface was always eroding in some places and building up in other places. This meant that Earth was much more than a few thousand years old. Now scientists know that Earth is more than four and a half billion years old.

Chapter Two

Ways to Study Rocks

Questions this chapter will answer:

- **What is rock?**
- **Rocks are made of minerals. How can you tell minerals apart?**
- **How can you tell real gold from fool's gold?**

You and Rockhound hike up into the Sierra Mountains in eastern California, where the California Gold Rush happened in the 1800s. You take your rock tools along.

Rockhound takes you to the mountains to look for gold.

"Keep an eye out for gold," says Rockhound. "You might get lucky and find it sitting right out on the ground!"

You walk for a while, and then suddenly you see it. "Gold!" you shout. "How much is this worth, Rockhound?"

Rockhound looks at the rock. He says, "Well, a chunk of gold this size could be worth hundreds of dollars, but not this one. It isn't worth anything at all. It's fool's gold. But I'll take it for my collection anyway."

Gold or fool's gold?

You take a long look at Rockhound. Is he really your friend, or is he cheating you out of your gold?

"Hold on," you say. "How do you know this isn't gold?"

Rockhound laughs. "Oh, I can tell rocks apart," he answers.

"Prove it," you say.

Rockhound sits down and explains what rocks are made of. He explains how to tell different rocks apart. This chapter tells you what he says.

What's in Rock?

Earth's crust is made of different kinds of rock. Different rocks are made of different **minerals**. You could say that minerals are the building blocks of rock. Some kinds of rock are just one kind of mineral, but most rocks are a mix of different minerals.

Minerals are made up of crystals. Crystals come in many different shapes and sizes. Sometimes the shape of the crystal can help you to know what kind of mineral you are looking at. Remember the crystals you found in the geode? They were large crystals of the mineral called **quartz**.

Very large crystals of pure quartz

You can find quartz all over the place if you look for it. Quartz crystals are almost clear and they have flat sides.

Mineral crystals can be smaller than the crystals in a geode. A magnifying glass can help you see the small crystals that are mixed together in rock.

This photo shows a piece of rock that is made of different kinds of minerals with different shapes and colors.

Telling Minerals Apart

Most metals are minerals. For example, copper and iron are minerals. So is gold.

There are tests to tell minerals apart. Look at the photos of the two minerals. One is gold. The other is fool's gold. Geologists call it **pyrite**.

This is gold.

This is fool's gold.

How can you tell which is which? Here are some of the questions that geologists ask to tell minerals apart:

- What color is the mineral?
- Does light shine through it?
- What shape are its crystals?
- How heavy is it?
- How hard is it?
- What happens when light hits it? For example, does it shine like metal? Does it look waxy or dull?

- What happens when you hit the mineral? Does it split apart, or does it break into thin splinters or little chips?
- Try the streak test. If you scrape the mineral across a white tile, what color is the streak that it makes on the tile?

Let's see what these tests say about your rock. Is it gold or fool's gold? Are you about to get rich?

Testing Gold and Fool's Gold

You can't tell gold from pyrite by looking at its color. And you can't tell by seeing if it shines like metal when light hits it. Both gold and pyrite have a gold color and both shine like metal.

What about the shape of the crystals? The crystals in your mineral are shaped like cubes. Pyrite has that kind of shape. Most gold does not look like that, but some gold does. So this test doesn't tell us anything for sure.

What about checking how heavy it is? Gold is heavier than pyrite, but you don't have a scale with you. So you can't do this test now.

What about hardness? Gold is soft. You can make a scratch in it with the point of a knife. You try this on your rock. You can only scratch it a little bit. You ask Rockhound what this means, but he just laughs and tells you to try the last few tests.

What happens when you break the rock? You hit the rock with your hammer, and the rock breaks into pieces. Too bad. Pyrite breaks like that, but real gold does not.

Now try the streak test. Rockhound takes out a tile that is made out of white clay, like the tiles you might find on the wall beside a bathtub. "Don't use the smooth side of the tile," says Rockhound. "Use the back." You scrape your rock across the tile and you look at the color of the streak. The streak is greenish black. Too bad again. A greenish black streak can mean fool's gold — pyrite — but it cannot mean gold. Gold would make a gold streak.

Better luck next time!

Pyrite makes a greenish black streak in the streak test.

"Here's one more test we could have used," says Rockhound. "My camping knife has a steel blade. Take the knife and hit the pyrite with it." Rockhound hands you his knife.

You hit the pyrite with the steel blade, and you see a spark.

"That means for sure that the rock is not gold," Rockhound explains. "Pyrite makes a spark with steel, but gold does not."

Chapter Summary

In this chapter, you learned that rocks are made of minerals. You can tell minerals apart with different tests. You can look at the color of the rock. You can see what happens when light hits it. You can also see whether light can shine through it. You can see how heavy it is, and how hard it is. You can look at the shape of its crystals. You can hit it with a hammer to see how it breaks. And you can try the streak test.

Some of these tests can tell you whether a mineral is real gold or fool's gold. The streak test and the spark tests will tell you for sure.

Chapter Three

Looking Underground at Layers of Earth

Questions this chapter will answer:

- **What are two tools that can be used to study deep strata of rock?**
- **What kind of rock starts out as sediment?**
- **What kind of rock starts out as hot melted rock?**
- **What is metamorphic rock?**

One day, Rockhound calls you on his cell phone, even though he's right outside.

"I'm going out with my crew to look for oil," he says. "Do you want to come along?"

You go outside to join him, and there you find the strangest truck that you have ever seen.

Rockhound drives up in his truck.

"Climb aboard," says Rockhound. "This baby can really shake!"

You ask, "Is that good?"

"Yeah," says Rockhound. "This truck was made to shake the ground like an earthquake. It tells us what is in the strata down below."

Rockhound drives out into the country. He turns into a field and parks there. Everyone gets out of the truck. Then, Rockhound and his crew lower a platform onto the ground from the middle of the truck. The whole truck is now sitting on top of the platform.

Rockhound yells to the crew, "Let her shake!"

The truck engine roars. The truck and the platform start to shake. The ground below you shakes, too.

Rockhound's truck is a tool for studying strata that are deep underground. How does it do that? What other ways can geologists study deep strata? And what kinds of rock do they find? This chapter answers these questions.

Two Tools for Looking Underground

Rockhound's truck is called a **vibrator truck**. A vibrator truck makes the ground shake like in an earthquake. The shaking goes deep into the ground. Geologists have special instruments that can measure the shaking to learn about the strata below the truck. They learn what is in the strata and how deep they are.

A vibrator truck

Another way that geologists study deep strata is to dig into the ground. If you pound a short piece of pipe into the ground, the pipe may be full of dirt when you pull it out. This is like the way geologists study the Earth's strata, but instead of a short pipe, they use a long hollow steel tube that's attached to a drill. The drill takes the hollow steel tube down into the ground. When the tube comes back up, it brings up a long sample of the layers that are deep underground. The sample of layers is called a **core sample**. The geologists empty the tube carefully so they don't change or break the order of the layers of rock in the core sample.

Core-sample drilling can go down very deep. In 1994, a core-sample hole went down more than 7 miles (11 kilometers). A hole all the way through Earth's crust would have to be about 40 to 50 miles (64 to 85 kilometers) deep.

Core samples show us many things. They show us how the surface of Earth has changed over billions of years. A core sample might tell a surprising story about the ground that is below the spot where you are sitting right now. The sample might show that your spot has been an ocean floor, then a desert, then a swamp, then another ocean, and then a desert again over many millions of years.

One core sample can be miles long. It can fill many boxes like this one.

In the rest of this chapter, you'll find out about the three main kinds of rock. They are called sedimentary rock, igneous rock, and metamorphic rock. Geologists might find layers of all three of these main kinds of rock in one core sample.

Sedimentary Rock (Rock That Is Formed by Sediment)

The first kind of rock is **sedimentary rock**, which makes up most of Earth's crust. This kind of rock starts out as sediment, which then dries and becomes hard. Some kinds of sedimentary rock start out as mud on the bottom of a river or a lake. Other kinds of sedimentary rock start out as sand on the bottom of an ocean or in a desert. And some kinds of sedimentary rock start out as rock that is broken into pebbles by a landslide. Or it may be broken up by the movement of a glacier (a huge mass of ice). Sedimentary rock can even start out as seashells and dead plants. Over a long time, the upper layers of sediment press down on the bottom layers and turn them into rock.

If the bottom layers of sediment are made of sand, we get sandstone, which is good for carving and for building. If the layers contain mostly seashells, then we get limestone, which is also used in building. And limestone is important for making cement and steel.

Limestone is crushed before it is used in making steel or cement.

If the layers of sediment are clay, then we get another kind of sedimentary rock called shale. Oil is often found between layers of shale, limestone, or sandstone, so geologists look for those rocks when they look for oil. Coal is another sedimentary rock, and it comes from thick layers of dead plants that have turned into rock after many, many years. Some coal began as forests more than 300 million years ago.

Igneous Rock (Rock That Is Formed by Fire)

The second main kind of rock on Earth is called **igneous rock**. The word *igneous* means "made by fire." Igneous rock is formed out of **magma**, which is hot, melted rock under Earth's crust. Igneous rock is formed when magma cools. Sometimes magma cools inside the ground and turns into igneous rock. And sometimes magma travels up through Earth's crust inside volcanoes. When magma spills out of volcanoes, it is called *lava*. When the lava cools, it turns into igneous rock.

Granite is a kind of igneous rock that is found in many places. If you want to see granite, go to Mount Rushmore in South Dakota. The faces of four presidents of the United States are carved in granite there. Granite is made of quartz and other minerals.

Mount Rushmore is made of granite.

Metamorphic Rock (Rock That Has Changed from One Kind to Another)

The third main kind of rock is called **metamorphic rock**. The name *metamorphic* means "changed in shape." Metamorphic rock starts out as sedimentary or igneous rock inside Earth's crust. But when sedimentary or igneous rock gets hot, and other heavy layers of rock press down on it, it turns into metamorphic rock.

Marble is a hard metamorphic rock that started out as limestone. Marble is great for carving statues. It can be polished to be as smooth as glass.

This floor is made of different colors of marble.

Chapter Summary

In this chapter, you learned about tools for studying strata that are deep underground. You also learned about the different kinds of rock that make up these strata. One tool for studying strata is a vibrator truck, which shakes the ground like an earthquake. A second tool is a drill that brings up core samples.

There are three main kinds of rock. Sedimentary rock is sediment that has become dry and hard. Igneous rock comes from magma. Metamorphic rock is igneous or sedimentary rock that is changed as it gets hot and as other heavy layers of rock press down on it. All these changes happen over thousands and thousands of years.

Chapter Four

Eyes in the Sky

Questions this chapter will answer:

- **Today we can see pictures of Earth that are taken from outer space. What do these pictures tell us about geology?**
- **What tool do geologists use to see how Earth's crust is moving?**

One day, Rockhound visits your school. One of the teachers has asked him to teach students about geology. Rockhound sees you in the hall.

"What's up?" he says. "Are you learning anything new about Earth these days?"

You say, "As a matter of fact, I've been looking at Earth from outer space. Come with me to the lab."

In the school science lab, you show Rockhound a computer. On the computer, he can see photos that were taken from high above Earth.

This photo taken from outer space shows farmland and mountains in California.

"Who got these pictures?" Rockhound asks.

"I guess you could say that I did," you tell him.

"You were in outer space?" says Rockhound. "I don't believe it!"

You say, "Of course I wasn't up there myself, but I sent questions to scientists who have a camera on the International Space Station. The scientists took these photos for me. Students do it at other schools, too. We are part of a program called EarthKAM."

These students are taking part in the EarthKAM program.

"Wow!" says Rockhound. "Photos from outer space can show us some interesting things about Earth."

Rockhound is right. This chapter talks about two kinds of tools that geologists use to study Earth from outer space.

Seeing Earth from Outer Space

Remember how James Hutton saw bent strata of rock that had become hills and mountains? Hutton could see a few hills from the surface of Earth. But from outer space we can see thousands of miles of hills or mountains.

We can get great photos of the face of Earth from cameras on the space station. We can also get great photos from **satellites** (spacecraft that are in orbit around Earth). Satellite photos help geologists make maps of Earth's surface. These photos can show changes in a river's shape after a big flood, and they can show changes in the surface of Earth after an earthquake. Satellite photos can also show different kinds of rock on Earth's surface. This helps geologists find oil and minerals under ground.

A satellite in orbit above Earth

Watching Earth's Crust Move

About 100 years ago, geologists began to figure out that the crust of Earth is broken into large flat pieces. These pieces are called **plates**. The plates of Earth's crust are slowly moving and sometimes they push against each other or pull apart. Sometimes we feel this movement as earthquakes. But even when we don't feel it, the plates are still moving.

Scientists have found a way to use satellites to tell them when a certain spot on Earth's surface has fallen, risen, or moved. They can get this information even when the spot has moved less than half an inch (less than one centimeter). They use a group of satellites called **GPS** to do this. GPS is made up of more than 20 satellites that are in orbit around Earth. These satellites send radio signals to stations all over Earth's surface.

Scientists use GPS receivers, like the one in the backpack, to measure changes in Earth's crust.

When a station on Earth receives signals from four satellites at the same time, scientists can tell exactly where that station is. Then they look to see where the station was the last time they sent signals to it. This tells the scientists if the ground at that station has moved up, down, or sideways.

Satellite photos and GPS let us see how Earth is changing. Now we don't need to wait a hundred or a thousand years to see changes in Earth's geology. We can see tiny changes as they happen from year to year.

Chapter Summary

In this chapter, you learned about tools in space that scientists use to study Earth's crust. Satellite photos let us see the crust in new ways — ways that we could never see it from the ground. GPS tells us exactly how much the plates of Earth's crust are moving.

Glossary

Word	Definition	Page
coal	a kind of **sedimentary rock** that is made from plants	33
core sample	a sample of rock **strata** obtained by drilling into Earth's **crust**	30
crust	the rocky outer layer of Earth	11
erode	to wear away rock or soil A river erodes its banks. Strong waves erode the cliffs by the ocean.	10
geode	a round, hollow rock with crystals inside	6
geologist	a scientist who studies Earth and its rocks	5
geology	the study of Earth and its rocks	5
GPS	a group of satellites that sends signals to stations on Earth Scientists use GPS to study Earth's movements. If you have GPS in your car, you are getting directions with the help of satellites in outer space.	41

Word	Definition	Page
granite	a very hard **igneous rock** that is found in many places.	34
igneous rock	the kind of rock that is made when **magma** cools	34
limestone	a kind of light-colored **sedimentary rock** that is formed at the bottom of an ocean	12
magma	hot melted rock that is under the surface of Earth	34
marble	a kind of **metamorphic rock** that started out as **limestone**	35
metamorphic rock	a kind of rock that is formed out of **sedimentary** or **igneous rock** deep inside Earth's crust	35
mineral	Rocks are made of minerals. Some kinds of rock are just one kind of mineral, but most rocks are a mix of different minerals.	21
plates	pieces of Earth's **crust**	41
pyrite	fool's gold	23

Word	Definition	Page
quartz	a **mineral** that is almost clear Quartz crystals have flat sides. Quartz is the most common mineral on earth.	21
sandstone	a kind of **sedimentary rock** that is formed out of sand	13
satellite	a spacecraft that is in orbit around Earth	40
sediment	bits of dirt, rock, and sand that are often found in the bottom of rivers, lakes and seas	10
sedimentary rock	the kind of rock that is made when **sediment** becomes hard	32
shale	a kind of **sedimentary rock** that is made from clay	33
strata	layers of rock in Earth's crust	12
vibrator truck	a special kind of truck that shakes Earth's **crust** to find out what kind of **strata** it has	29

About the Author

Alan Venable grew up in Pittsburgh, Pennsylvania. After college, he was a teacher in Africa and traveled in other parts of the world. He has written many books for Start-to-Finish, as well as plays, novels, and children's books. He has two children and lives in an old house in San Francisco, California.

About the Narrator

John Sterchi has acted in movies, in plays, and in commercials. He has won awards for his acting and he was once in a movie with Tom Hanks! He has also narrated more than 300 books. John likes fishing, taking photos, watching basketball, and he's been to the Indy 500 eighteen times! John lives in Chicago with his two turtles, George and Lennie.

A Note to the Teacher

Start-to-Finish Core Content books are designed to help students achieve success in reading to learn. From the provocative cover question to the carefully structured and considerate text, these books promote inquiry, active engagement, and understanding. Not only do students learn curriculum-relevant content, but they learn how to read with understanding. Here are some of the features that make these books such powerful aids in teaching and learning.

Structure That Supports Inquiry and Understanding

Core Content books are carefully structured to encourage students to ask questions, identify main ideas, and understand how ideas relate to one another. The structural features of the Blue Core Content books include the following:

- **"Introduction":** A concise introduction engages students in the book's topic and explicitly states the book's themes.
- **Clearly focused chapters:** Each of the following chapters focuses on a single topic at a length that makes for a comfortable session of reading.
- **"Questions This Chapter Will Answer":** Provocative questions following the chapter title reflect the chapter's main ideas. Each question corresponds to a heading within the chapter.
- **Chapter introduction:** An engaging opening leads to a clear statement of the chapter topic.
- **Carefully worded headings:** The headings within each chapter are carefully worded to signal the main idea of the section and reflect the opening questions.
- **Clear topic statements:** Within each chapter section, the main idea is explicitly stated so that students can distinguish it from supporting details.
- **"Chapter Summary":** A brief summary recaptures the main ideas signaled by the opening questions, text headings, and topic statements.

Text That Is Written for Success™

Every page of a Core Content book is the product of a skilled team of educators, writers, and editors who understand your students' needs. The text features of these books include the following:

- **Mature treatment of grade level curriculum:** Core Content is age and grade-appropriate for the older student who is actively acquiring reading skills. The books also contain information that may be new to any student in the class, empowering Core Content readers to contribute interesting information to class discussions.
- **Idioms and vocabulary:** The text limits the density of new vocabulary and carefully introduces new words, new meanings of familiar words, and idioms. New subject-specific terms are bold-faced and included in the Glossary.
- **Background knowledge:** The text assumes little prior knowledge and anchors the reader using familiar examples and analogies.
- **Sentence structure:** Blue level text introduces a greater variety of complex sentences than are used at the easier Gold level to help students make a transition to the language of traditional textbooks.

For More Information

To find out more about Start-to-Finish Core Content, visit www.donjohnston.com for full product information, standards and research base.